EVAN PLACEY

Evan Placey is a Canadian-British playwright who grew up in Toronto and now lives in London, England. His plays include *Mother of Him* (Courtyard Theatre; winner of the King's Cross Award for New Writing, RBC National Playwriting Competition, Canada, and the Samuel French Canadian Play Contest); *Banana Boys* (Hampstead Theatre); *Suicide(s) in Vegas* (Canadian tour; Centaur Theatre Award nomination); *Scarberia* (Forward Theatre Project/York Theatre Royal); *How Was It For You?* (Unicorn Theatre); *Holloway Jones* (Synergy Theatre Project/schools tour/Unicorn Theatre; winner of the Brian Way Award 2012 for Best Play for Young People; Writers' Guild Award nomination); *Girls Like That* (Synergy/Unicorn Theatre; first produced and commissioned by Birmingham Repertory Theatre, Theatre Royal Plymouth and West Yorkshire Playhouse; winner of the Writers' Guild Award for Best Play for Young Audiences) and *Pronoun* (National Theatre Connections). Work for radio includes *Mother of Him* (BBC Radio 3/Little Brother Productions).

Evan is a Creative Fellow and Lecturer at the University of Southampton, and also teaches playwriting to young people for various theatres, and also in prisons.

Other Titles in this Series

Adam Barnard
BUCKETS

Mike Bartlett
BULL
GAME
AN INTERVENTION
KING CHARLES III

Tom Basden
THE CROCODILE
HOLES
JOSEPH K
THERE IS A WAR

Deborah Bruce
THE DISTANCE
GODCHILD
SAME

Jez Butterworth
JERUSALEM
JEZ BUTTERWORTH PLAYS: ONE
MOJO
THE NIGHT HERON
PARLOUR SONG
THE RIVER
THE WINTERLING

Caryl Churchill
BLUE HEART
CHURCHILL PLAYS: THREE
CHURCHILL PLAYS: FOUR
CHURCHILL: SHORTS
CLOUD NINE
DING DONG THE WICKED
A DREAM PLAY
    after Strindberg
DRUNK ENOUGH TO SAY
    I LOVE YOU?
FAR AWAY
HOTEL
ICECREAM
LIGHT SHINING IN
    BUCKINGHAMSHIRE
LOVE AND INFORMATION
MAD FOREST
A NUMBER
SEVEN JEWISH CHILDREN
THE SKRIKER
THIS IS A CHAIR
THYESTES *after* Seneca
TRAPS

Vivienne Franzmann
MOGADISHU
PESTS
THE WITNESS

debbie tucker green
BORN BAD
DIRTY BUTTERFLY
HANG
NUT
RANDOM
STONING MARY
TRADE & GENERATIONS
TRUTH AND RECONCILIATION

Stacey Gregg
LAGAN
OVERRIDE
PERVE
SHIBBOLETH
WHEN COWS GO BOOM

Sam Holcroft
COCKROACH
DANCING BEARS
EDGAR & ANNABEL
PINK
RULES FOR LIVING
THE WARDROBE
WHILE YOU LIE

Vicky Jones
THE ONE

Lucy Kirkwood
BEAUTY AND THE BEAST
    with Katie Mitchell
BLOODY WIMMIN
CHIMERICA
HEDDA *after* Ibsen
IT FELT EMPTY WHEN THE
    HEART WENT AT FIRST BUT
    IT IS ALRIGHT NOW
NSFW
TINDERBOX

Chloë Moss
CHRISTMAS IS MILES AWAY
HOW LOVE IS SPELT
FATAL LIGHT
THE GATEKEEPER
THE WAY HOME
THIS WIDE NIGHT

Evan Placey
GIRLS LIKE THAT
GIRLS LIKE THAT & OTHER PLAYS
    FOR TEENAGERS
PRONOUN

Stef Smith
REMOTE
SWALLOW

Jack Thorne
2ND MAY 1997
BUNNY
BURYING YOUR BROTHER IN
    THE PAVEMENT
HOPE
JACK THORNE PLAYS: ONE
LET THE RIGHT ONE IN
    after John Ajvide Lindqvist
MYDIDAE
STACY & FANNY AND FAGGOT
THE SOLID LIFE OF SUGAR WATER
WHEN YOU CURE ME

Phoebe Waller-Bridge
FLEABAG

Tom Wells
JUMPERS FOR GOALPOSTS
THE KITCHEN SINK
ME, AS A PENGUIN

Evan Placey

CONSENSUAL

NICK HERN BOOKS
London
www.nickhernbooks.co.uk

A Nick Hern Book

Consensual first published in Great Britain as a paperback original in 2015 by Nick Hern Books Limited, The Glasshouse, 49a Goldhawk Road, London W12 8QP

Consensual copyright © 2015 Evan Placey

Evan Placey has asserted his right to be identified as the author of this work

Cover photograph by Helen Maybanks

Designed and typeset by Nick Hern Books, London
Printed in the UK by Mimeo Ltd, Huntingdon, Cambridgeshire PE29 6XX

A CIP catalogue record for this book is available from the British Library

ISBN 978 1 84842 520 0

Consensual was first performed by the National Youth Theatre of Great Britain at Ambassadors Theatre, London, on 18 September 2015. The cast was as follows:

DIANE	Lauren Lyle
FREDDIE	Oscar Porter-Brentford
GEORGIA	Grace Surey
MARY	Megan Parkinson
PETE	Conor Neaves
JAKE	Cole Edwards
MR ABRAMOVICH	Oliver West

STUDENTS

BRANDON	Luke Pierre
RHYS	Gavi Singh Chera
NATHAN	Jason Imlach
OWEN	Oliver West
LIAM	Andrew Hanratty
GRACE	Francene Turner
TAYLOR	Melissa Taylor
KAYLA	Alice Feetham
DESTINY	Paris Iris Campbell
AMANDA	Ellise Chappell

Consensual was commissioned by NYT Artistic Director and CEO Paul Roseby.

Director	Pia Furtado
Assistant Director	Matt Harrison
Designer	Cecilia Carey
Production Manager	Alan Kingsley-Dobson
Technical Manager	Jackson Ingle
Company Stage Manager	Nick Hill
Musical Director	Jim Hustwit
Sound Designer	Emma Laxton
Sound Operator	Rich Price
Lighting Designer	Josh Pharo
Lighting Operator	Gareth Weaver
Head of Costume	Richard Gellar
Deputy Head of Costume	Elle Van Riel
Wardrobe Mistress	Katherine Hutchinson
Wardrobe Mistress	Ugne Dainiute
Producer	Beth Watling

national® youth theatre

The National Youth Theatre of Great Britain (NYT) is a world-leading youth arts organisation. NYT were established in 1956 as the first youth theatre in the world and have performed critically acclaimed productions over the past fifty-nine years. 2016 will be a celebration of their sixtieth year.

NYT's training is unique because they believe that the best place for young performers to learn is on stage in front of an audience. NYT showcase young talent on West End stages, in stadiums worldwide and at iconic sites both at home and abroad. They commission brave and relevant new writing and reinterpret classic stories for our time. They are as ambitious as the young people they serve.

NYT's world renowned alumni include: Helen Mirren, Daniel Craig, Chiwetel Ejiofor, Colin Firth, Rosamund Pike, Daniel Day-Lewis, Orlando Bloom, Catherine Tate, Ben Kingsley, Ashley Jensen, Derek Jacobi, Timothy Dalton, Zawe Ashton, Matt Lucas, Hugh Bonneville, Matt Smith and many more.

For more information visit **www.nyt.org.uk**

Characters

DIANE, *twenty-nine* (*and twenty-two*)
FREDDIE, *twenty-two* (*and fifteen*)
GEORGIA, *fifteen*
MARY, *twenty-three, pastoral assistant*
PETE, *thirty-six, Diane's husband*
JAKE, *twenty-two, Freddie's brother*
MR ABRAMOVICH

STUDENTS, *all fifteen years old*
NATHAN
BRANDON
RHYS
LIAM
OWEN
GRACE
AMANDA
TAYLOR
DESTINY
KAYLA

A Note on Punctuation

A dash (–) is a cut-off, sometimes of one's own thought with a different thought (not a pause or beat).

An ellipsis (…) is a loss or search for words.

A lack of punctuation at the end of a line means the next line comes right in.

A Note on Staging

Throughout Part One, the students should all be present in some way; perhaps watching the action or only there at the start and end of scenes, but their energy and lingering presence should be felt.

They are not present for Part Two.

Acknowledgements

Thank you Paul and Beth at the National Youth Theatre for the challenge.

Thank you especially to Pia Furtado.

E.P.

This text went to press before the end of rehearsals and so may differ slightly from the play as performed.

PART ONE: AFTER

Prologue

The STUDENTS, *in uniform, invade the stage. They're chatty, noisy. One of the* STUDENTS *has started beatboxing and the others have joined in singing. Despite the slight chaos of the scene, there's a unity to the singing. Even the kids who wouldn't normally be part of the crowd singing are enjoying themselves. There's also chatter over the top of and during the singing. There's something about their energy that's animal, that's frightening, that's sexy.*

And then all at once, the STUDENTS *simultaneously stop singing/talking as they turn to look at:*

Scene One

A pub. Afternoon.

DIANE *and* FREDDIE *sit at a table across from each other.* DIANE *is seven months pregnant.*

DIANE *sips a tea,* FREDDIE *a pint of beer.*

FREDDIE. You been to those classes, learn how to do nappies and that?

DIANE. No.

FREDDIE. You not worried you gonna put it on backwards or something?

DIANE. It's not my first.

FREDDIE. Oh right. How old is…?

DIANE. Why are we here?

FREDDIE. You chose it.

DIANE. I don't mean the place.

FREDDIE. Bit of a shithole if you don't mind me saying.

DIANE. Why would I mind?

FREDDIE. Just in case it's like your favourite pub or something.

DIANE. I've never been here before.

FREDDIE. Just thought since you

Oh, right. Right.

DIANE. What?

FREDDIE. Nothing. (*Smiles*.)

DIANE. Sorry your tie's gone to waste.

FREDDIE. Nah, it's my work ensemble. Barclays.

Why is that funny?

DIANE. It's not.

FREDDIE. You don't think I'm smart enough to work in a bank?

DIANE. I didn't... Freddie, why are we here?

FREDDIE. No one calls me that. Not a kid any more. 'S Frederick now.

DIANE. Frederick. Who works in a bank. In his ensemble.

FREDDIE. Are you making fun of me?

DIANE. No.

Yes. (*Laughs*.) Just doesn't seem like...

It's not you.

FREDDIE. How would you know? You don't know me any more.

DIANE. No. You're right.

Beat.

FREDDIE (*laughs*). Christ, it's so not me. (*Takes his tie off.*)

Sometimes catch myself in the mirror and it's like who's the kid who's come to work in their dad's clothes. (*Unbuttons shirt.*) Just something for the moment, get some experience, try to realise all that unfulfilled potential everyone was always telling me I had.

By now he's taken off his shirt and hung it with his tie over the chair and sits in a vest. DIANE, *uncomfortable, focuses on his face so as to not look at his body.*

There's kids, right, thirteen, fourteen, fifteen, starting businesses in their bedrooms, and they're bringing in thousands, only just getting their first pubes and they're like CEOs. I'm only twenty-two but I got like years to catch up on those little bed-wetters. And what if I'd done that. Do that a lot. *Maybe if, what if,* undo all the regrets in my head and see where I'd end up. Like this – (*Stands, pulls up his vest to show a scar just below his belly button.*) See that? Some stupid bar scrap when I was nineteen, don't even remember what it was about but ended up with piece of beer glass here. Can you see how there's no hair on that bit, like this sudden gap in the trail, and what if I'd just gone home, not ordered that extra pint?

He can see she's uncomfortable, pulls his vest back down.

DIANE. You need to say it. You have to actually say it, Freddie. Frederick.

FREDDIE. Say what?

DIANE. You have to actually say sorry. You can't just say there's regrets. You have to –

FREDDIE. Say sorry for what?

Pause.

Say sorry for what?

DIANE. Why did you text me? Why after seven years did you tell me we needed to meet? We *had* to meet?

Beat. She looks at her watch.

FREDDIE. You still got twenty minutes.

Lunch still ends at 1:25. I checked.

DIANE. I don't work there any more.

FREDDIE. No?

DIANE. I left. After... Maybe you didn't notice. But I left.

FREDDIE. I noticed. I missed you. Me and all the other retards.

DIANE. Don't –

FREDDIE. We did though.

DIANE. You're not a

FREDDIE. I am. Well, I was. Remember seeing my photo up on the staffroom wall. 'At risk' it said above our mug shots, me and all the other retards. Though at risk of what it didn't say.

DIANE. It's not a very nice word.

FREDDIE. Where do you work now?

DIANE. For an environmental company. A charity. We run campaigns. Get people to think about how they can modify their behaviour, in really practical ways, to lower their carbon footprint.

FREDDIE. Oh. Right. And does it change things? One person with a thermal mug, a bag for life?

DIANE. Yes.

I don't know.

Maybe – it's depressing – but maybe one person doesn't have an impact. Maybe all they have is a tiny little imprint.

FREDDIE. But multiple imprints eventually make a dent. And people take notice.

Beat. This has hit something in her. It's become suddenly intimate.

DIANE. I should go. I need, I need to go.

FREDDIE. To work?

DIANE. Yes. No. Yes.

I don't work for an environmental charity.

FREDDIE. What do you mean?

DIANE. I made it up.

FREDDIE. Why would you make that up?

DIANE. I don't know.

FREDDIE. Were you afraid I was going to show up there? Because if that's what I'd wanted to do, if that's the kind of person I am, I would have done that already.

DIANE. You know I didn't go back there.

FREDDIE. Not while I was there, no. Not as a pastoral assistant, no.

You did a PGCE then went back as a geography teacher

You married Pete, wore your hair in a braid for the wedding

You honeymooned on the Amalfi Coast

You briefly dyed your hair brown

You still wear that red cardigan even though it doesn't fit as well

You're head of Year 10

Three years ago you became a vegetarian

Last weekend you baked peanut-butter cookies

You do think no one cares about how we're destroying the planet, but you don't work for an environmental charity.

Beat. She stands to leave.

Where are you going? It's still sixteen minutes before next lesson.

DIANE. What is this, Freddie, Frederick? You're stalking me?

FREDDIE. Did you never look me up? Never on a bored Saturday afternoon, just wonder… does he have a girlfriend? A goatee? Just do a harmless Twitter or Facebook search?

DIANE. No.

I shouldn't have come.

Goodbye, Freddie.

FREDDIE. My dad died.

A glass somewhere in the bar breaks. They both watch.

DIANE *sits.*

DIANE. I'm sorry.

FREDDIE. A week ago. Bastard finally drank himself to death.

You probably don't remember, but one time, we were in your office. I was crying. Told you my mum was gone, had a brother who did fuck-all, and had a dad who didn't love me. And you told me he did, of course he did. He was just too afraid to show it. You probably don't remember.

DIANE. I remember.

FREDDIE. The night he died he's lying in hospital drugged-up and he takes my hands. Like properly takes them. (*Takes her hands.*) And he says, swear to god, 'I love you, son. I know I was never very good at sayin' it. Maybe cos my dad never said it to me, so was too scared to. But I love you.

Jake. I love you, Jake. Not like that faggot brother of yours. I tried, god knows I tried. But the thing with Freddie is he wants it too much. You can smell it when he walks into a room. He just so desperately wants to be loved that I couldn't stand to look at him. Like one of them manky wet foxes you'd find by the bins, staring up at you, longing in their eyes. Just makes you want to kick the shit out of them.'

Pause.

Dad was right. People can smell it on me. The fellas at work always taking the mick cos they know I'll take it. My last girlfriend who told me I was too needy.

So how did you know?

DIANE. Know what?

FREDDIE. How did you, why did you choose me?

DIANE. I don't know what you mean.

FREDDIE. Dammit, can you just – ! If I knew what it is that people see in me, what they smell on me that –

If I knew what you saw in me so you knew you could...

DIANE. Could what?

FREDDIE. You know.

DIANE. No. I don't, Freddie.

FREDDIE. Groom me. If I knew what it was that you saw, so that you knew that you could groom me, that you could...

She laughs incredulously.

DIANE. Are you insane? Freddie? Are you insane?

FREDDIE. No.

DIANE. You think I – ?! You actually think –

FREDDIE. I don't *think* anything. I remember.

DIANE. What do you remember, Freddie?

FREDDIE. Got me to trust you. You made it so I became dependent on you. So you could exploit that trust, that dependency. And take advantage of me.

DIANE. *You* showed up at *my* house.

FREDDIE. You gave me your number.

DIANE. *You* came on to *me*.

FREDDIE. You told me I had a good body. Told me to get undressed. You got me drunk and then had sex with me.

DIANE. I'm pretty sure you got what you wanted. And then some, as I remember it.

FREDDIE. It doesn't matter what I wanted. What I *thought* I wanted. I wasn't old enough to know, to properly understand, miss.

DIANE. Don't you '*miss*' me. Don't you dare

FREDDIE. I was fifteen.

DIANE. Sixteen.

FREDDIE. You know I wasn't.

DIANE. Don't tell me what I know.

FREDDIE. You bought me things.

DIANE. I didn't buy you anything.

FREDDIE. I still have it.

DIANE. Have what?

FREDDIE. The bracelet.

He pulls out a threaded bracelet. Lays it on the table between them. She stares at it like it's going to ignite.

Do you know what's most pathetic of all, miss? How even after – I kept texting you. You never replied, but still I, for months. Didn't come back to school once you'd got what you wanted from me, but even when you'd tossed me aside, even when I felt sick cos of what we did that night, still like a loyal little cunt I didn't tell no one, kept texting to see if you were alright – that's how well you groomed me.

DIANE. I think you're right. You are a retard. You truly have some kind of mental retardation.

I'm sorry your dad was an abusive alcoholic who didn't love you. I'm sorry you have a shitty job in a bank with co-workers who don't like you. Mostly I'm sorry that seven years later and you're still the same sixteen-year-old who's blaming others for your problems. But I'm not sorry for something that never happened. So if that was why you contacted me, if that's what you thought would fix your life, I can't give you that.

FREDDIE. I went to the police. I made a statement. Maybe nothing will happen, it will just be an imprint. Or maybe it will make a dent. But I thought I should tell you. That that would be the adult thing to do.

Scene Two

A classroom. Same afternoon.

On the board is a large drawing of a penis a student has put there. Teacherless, the STUDENTS *sit on desks, wheel around on teacher's chair, etc. All the* STUDENTS, *minus* GRACE *and* LIAM, *are present.* OWEN *sleeps, his cap pulled down low.*

DIANE *enters.*

BRANDON. You late, miss. Gotta get a note from the office innit?

DIANE. Rhys, can I have my chair back.

BRANDON. We thought you wasn't coming, miss.

RHYS. What you talking 'bout her cumming for?

DIANE. Rhys, my chair. 10B, we're starting.

DESTINY. How come you is late, miss? Form half over.

    DIANE *counts them all, ticks the register.*

TAYLOR. Miss? (*Giggles.*) Um, miss?

DIANE. What is it, Taylor?

TAYLOR. Um like… have you looked behind you?

DIANE. Are you referring to the large erect penis behind me?

TAYLOR. Aren't you gonna rub it out?

BRANDON. D'you just ask her if she's gonna rub one out?

DIANE. No. To both questions.

TAYLOR. Just really distracting.

DIANE. Tell that to whoever's put it there. Right, we don't have long. Um. (*Pulls out lesson plan.*) Today we're starting our new SRE unit.

KAYLA. What's SRE again?

RHYS. We've only been doing it since Year 7.

BRANDON. I've definitely been doing it since Year 7 if you get me.

AMANDA. Sex and Relationships Education.

KAYLA. Oh my gosh, it is like too soon after lunch for this.

DIANE. Taylor, put away your phone please.

KAYLA. Honestly, miss. I can't be dealing with this right now.

DIANE. Dealing with what exactly, Kayla?

RHYS. Yeah, you're the cock expert, Kayla.

DIANE (*trying to get PowerPoint to work*). Right so we're… um… why isn't this working?

RHYS. You want me to plug you in, miss?

DESTINY. Nasty.

DIANE. Rhys, have you been fiddling with this?

KAYLA. He's just been fiddling with himself.

DESTINY. Booyaka!

GRACE *and* LIAM *enter.*

LIAM. Sorry we're late.

BRANDON. They were getting a head start on the sex education.

RHYS. I can smell it.

DIANE. We'll use an old-fashioned marker. (*Writes up 'Healthy Relationships'.*)

DESTINY. We already did this, miss.

DIANE. No we have not.

DESTINY. Yes we did, didn't we? You made us think of a word we thought described a healthy relationship.

DIANE. In preparation of this. So. What words did people think of?…

Did anyone do the homework?…

Perhaps we can just do it now. Ideas? On what makes a relationship healthy?

Silence.

The point is for you all to have a discussion. Of what you think.

RHYS. Sex. Obviously.

AMANDA. I think honesty is most important. Because without complete transparency in a relationship nothing else works – including sex.

BRANDON. Have you had sex? Has she had sex?

TAYLOR. Owen's snoring in my ear.

DESTINY. Can I just say, miss, that I disagree with Amanda. Cos sometimes it's good to have secrets, like I don't want some boy knowing everything about my business, you get me? Just cos he in my bed don't mean he has to be all up in my head!

KAYLA. Ohhh, snap!

RHYS. How often is a healthy amount of times to have sex, miss?

GRACE. That's different for everyone, isn't it?

RHYS. I want a number though. Miss, how often do you and your husband have sex?

AMANDA. Rhys. That's not appropriate.

RHYS. Why isn't that appropriate? Miss, is that inappropriate?

AMANDA. Yes.

RHYS. How come?

KAYLA. Because she's a teacher innit.

BRANDON. And can't be making assumptions, maybe she's not had sex.

AMANDA. Obviously she'd had sex.

BRANDON. How do you know?

AMANDA. Because she's pregnant.

BRANDON. Maybe it was IVF though.

LIAM. It's not about how often. It's about it being good. Good sex. Like my parents have sex sometimes

DESTINY. Nasty

LIAM. So did yours. But that doesn't necessarily mean their relationship is healthy.

AMANDA. Miss?

Miss Andrews?

Though DIANE*'s been staring ahead the whole time, she's clearly been somewhere else.*

DIANE. Yes. Amanda.

AMANDA. Nathan's had his hand up for a while.

DIANE. Oh. It's a… discussion, Nathan. You can just speak.

NATHAN. I don't have a point of view on the secrets thing or sex thing but I think it's really important to acknowledge that we're taking a really heteronormative view of all this.

KAYLA. Oh my days.

DIANE. That's a… good point.

Perhaps now would be a good time to do our first worksheet. (*Looks at notes.*) There are various scenarios and you move them into the healthy or unhealthy column. And then we'll… discuss. Right, have a go.

Pause.

TAYLOR. Miss?

DIANE. What is it?

TAYLOR. We don't have any worksheets.

DIANE. Yes. Good point. (*Smiles.*)

And it seems… (*Keeps searching.*) that I left them in the office…

In which case does anyone have anything else they'd like to add?

RHYS. About what?

DIANE. About. What we were just talking about.

RHYS. About honesty?

DIANE. Yes.

RHYS. Or about sex?

DIANE. Either. Both.

BRANDON. Sometimes it's good to be dishonest. Like when you're having sex and picturing someone else. Should you tell them that?

GRACE. If you're picturing someone else then it's probably not very healthy.

BRANDON. You think Liam's never pictured anyone else?

GRACE. No.

BRANDON. Lies. Liam?

LIAM. No.

BRANDON. Do you see how he hesitated?

And also. I think like you gotta keep secrets if you don't like like something they're doing to you in bed? Cos it might hurt their feelings. Like sometimes you know how a girl slips you the finger back there.

RHYS. You are so gay.

BRANDON. How is that gay?

RHYS. Some girl's putting her finger up your arse!

BRANDON. That's where the male G-spot is.

RHYS. You're gay.

Nathan, he's gay, right?

BRANDON. I'm not putting a dick up my ass. It's just a finger or some beads.

KAYLA. Oh. My. Days. My precious ears.

BRANDON. What I'm saying is even if you don't like something you don't wanna like tell them cos might hurt their feelings so you just gotta like go along with it.

AMANDA. That sounds a bit rapey to me.

BRANDON. What you talking about, fool?

AMANDA. Well, you're saying if two people are having sex and one of them doesn't like something that they should just suck it up or whatever. That not only sounds unhealthy, that sounds a bit like sexual assault.

BRANDON. How is it sexual assault if it's with your girlfriend?

AMANDA. People can still be assaulted or raped in a relationship?

It's called consent.

NATHAN. None of us can actually give consent because we're not yet sixteen. It's actually illegal for us to have sex.

RHYS. What's Tom Daley talking about?

NATHAN. You are not old enough to give consent. And if you're having sex with someone underage then she or he can't give consent either.

RHYS. You saying I'm a paedo?

TAYLOR. They going to prison, miss?

DIANE. No one's. Going to prison. They don't. Enforce the law on young people having sex.

RHYS. So then why do they have the law?

DESTINY. To protect us from creepy fifty-year-old men online pretending they're fourteen.

GRACE. I think the age of consent should be lowered.

DESTINY. Course you do, cos your gohno-mouth is a daily crime scene.

GRACE. I think that we all mature differently and we should be able to decide when we're able to consent to sex, not the government.

BRANDON. Should be when you hit puberty innit?

DESTINY. Guess that's like another ten years before you can have it then.

BRANDON. That's funny, flappy fanny.

DESTINY. Eat me.

BRANDON. I would but hear Samuel Canning already doing that.

DESTINY. Kayla!

KAYLA. What? I didn't tell him.

LIAM. What do you think, miss? Should the age of consent be lowered?

DIANE. Um, well that's not really what we're talking about.

KAYLA. It's like literally what we're talking about right now.

DIANE. There is a lesson in a couple of weeks when we shall certainly talk about consent. And the age of and I think right now we should focus on...

LIAM. Do you think we're wrong, miss?

DIANE. I'm not entirely sure what you're

LIAM. Do you think it's wrong for people our age to have sex?

DIANE. ...No.

GRACE. So we should be able to consent, right?

DIANE. Probably. Yes. I mean. No. It depends.

GRACE. Depends on what?

DIANE. We should really save this for our...

Looking at you I would say you seem able to make a decision of what's right for you. That you would know if you're ready and know what you're doing. So... yes. But for others...

Nathan, you don't need to put your hand up.

NATHAN. But then who decides?

DIANE. Who decides what?

NATHAN. If someone knows what they're doing. If they're ready. Who decides if they're able to consent?

Pause.

A knock at the door.

DIANE. Hello, Ms Willis.

MARY. Sorry to interrupt, just, there's a phone call for you.

DIANE. You'll have to take a message. Tell them I'm in form, where you should be as well.

MARY. It's just… he says it's important…

DIANE. Well, who is it?

MARY. It's um… a Detective Tyler?

RHYS. Boom!

Scene Three

DIANE *and* PETE*'s house.*

PETE. If they were going to arrest you, then they would have.

DIANE. You think?

PETE. Yes. Probably.

DIANE. Probably?

PETE. Did they say it was under caution?

DIANE. I don't remember.

PETE. I wish you'd called a solicitor.

DIANE. They just said they wanted to ask me some questions. I think that was all they said. And I said, what I told you.

They just said they were following up a. There had been an accusation against me. They wanted to ask me some questions. That's all.

Maybe they did. Maybe they did say under caution.

PETE. Next time call a solicitor.

DIANE. What next time?

And how does one even call a solicitor? Just look a random one up in the phone book?

PETE. I work with solicitors all the time.

DIANE. You think your tax buddies are going to be any help to me? *Yes it's possible she coerced him into sex but we can say for certain she paid her taxes.*

PETE. I'm trying to help.

Pause.

DIANE. Am I going to prison?

Beat.

You haven't even asked me.

PETE. You just told me.

DIANE. I told you what I told the police.

PETE. That's enough for me. It doesn't matter to me.

DIANE. It doesn't matter? It doesn't matter if I'm a paedophile?

PETE. You're being silly now.

DIANE. But that's what they'll say. That's what this is.

Seven years his senior.

PETE. I'm seven years your senior.

DIANE. And was that part of it? The attraction? My being a vulnerable naive young twenty-two-year-old that you could have power over?

PETE. No. And I don't know where this is coming from.

DIANE. No. Because you're not that sort of man.

PETE. No. I'm not.

DIANE. He'd appear like this abandoned mutt that's gotten its leash caught in your back-garden fence. And you give him a little bit of food, brush his fur and soon he won't leave. And pretty soon he gets strong enough he starts biting, and pissing on the couches, but still all you allow yourself to see is the poor mutt that couldn't find its way home.

I just didn't want to abandon him lest all the hard work I'd put into him go to waste.

PETE. You care too much. It's why I fell in love with you. And they'll have seen that, that it's all the deluded fantasies of a deranged kid blaming the one person who tried to help him.

DIANE. What if it's not a delusion?

He came to my flat. I didn't tell them that. But he did, Pete. I can't remember if I gave him my address for emergencies or – because he had this violent dad – and probably I shouldn't have, if I did at all, but the kid had no one. And he came to my flat. And I was drunk. Very drunk. I'd been out. And.

I don't remember what happened.

PETE. When was this?

DIANE. Shortly before I left the job.

PETE. When we started going out.

DIANE. Yes, maybe. No. Before that. I'm not sure.

PETE. So he came over. And what happened?

DIANE. I don't remember.

PETE. If you don't remember –

DIANE. I don't.

PETE. Are you saying he, that he

DIANE. No. No. I'm saying. No, we didn't, Pete, I didn't, I'm saying it doesn't matter. Because it can still be grooming without sex. That's what they said.

PETE. You didn't say that before.

DIANE. I just remembered.

PETE. When did they say that?

DIANE. After I said. After I said I didn't have sex with him.

After I asked if there was some sort of… evidence?

PETE. You didn't say that before.

DIANE. Well, I'm saying it now. And they said no.

And I said well, it didn't happen, so that should be the end of things.

And they said, that it doesn't necessarily matter about the sex. That it's the *intention*.

Asking me if I ever talked to him about his personal life, or mine. I was a pastoral assistant – it was my bloody job to talk to kids about their personal lives! Every day kids tell me about some video they saw on the internet, or their parents divorce or friend's abortion, and I'm meant to teach them about bullying and peer pressure and alcohol and porn and gonorrhoea – seeing them more hours every day than their own parents, but I'm meant to do that without ever getting personal, lest something be misconstrued.

PETE. I hope that's not what you said.

DIANE. I said of course at times it was necessary to speak about my own life – an anecdote or – But that the only *intention* was to help a troubled young man.

They could put me on the sex-offenders register, Pete. They could take away Maddie and. (*Touches stomach.*) All because of some attention-seeking – why is he doing this? Why me? Us?

PETE. It will go away.

DIANE. You need to make it.

PETE. It already has. How could anyone think of you as a predator?

DIANE. You're not listening to me. Your daughter will be born in a cell.

I know this kid. And he won't roll over if he doesn't get a biscuit.

Make it go away, Pete.

PETE. I'll take care of it.

DIANE. Do you promise?

PETE. Yes.

Beat. DIANE *picks up a naked Barbie from the floor, begins to clothe it.*

DIANE. Where did you tell Maddie I was this evening?

PETE. She didn't ask. Think she was relieved. Had to see the headteacher today.

DIANE. Why?

PETE. She stole someone's crisps. Apparently she didn't want her organic rice cakes. Hid the crisps in her pants, but forgot about them, and they fell out during PE.

DIANE *starts laughing about it. They both do.*

DIANE. Guess I'm not the only one facing prison.

What? It was a joke.

(*Hearing movement above.*) I think we woke her.

PETE. Do you want to check?

DIANE. You go.

He exits. DIANE *stares into the dark through a window. Flicks on the outside light.* FREDDIE *is standing there. She turns off the light again.* (*He's not actually there.*)

Scene Four

Three weeks later. A small mechanics garage.

JAKE *is working on the body of a car.* FREDDIE *stands with coffee and doughnuts.*

FREDDIE. She's nice.

JAKE. Where've you been, Fred?

FREDDIE. Yeah sorry.

JAKE. Meant to come by like three weeks ago to help go through Dad's stuff. Don't pick up your phone.

FREDDIE. Yeah sorry.

JAKE. And the probate guy's being a pain in the arse, needs us both there for the will. And looks like there's probably bills and stuff of his we'll need to take care of. You speak to your buddies at the bank?

FREDDIE. Yeah. Yeah, course. They're looking into it. Just behind on other applications.

JAKE. You're full of shit.

FREDDIE. Jake.

JAKE. You didn't talk to no one.

FREDDIE. I will.

JAKE. Cos if you can't actually, I don't know why you'd tell me that. Why you'd make something like that up.

FREDDIE. I will, Jake. Just been a bit of a. I sent you an email. Three weeks ago.

You didn't... respond. Except your 'Come by' text this morning, you haven't actually...

JAKE. I deleted it.

Beat.

What the fuck you gone and got yourself into now, Freddie?

FREDDIE. I dunno what you mean.

JAKE. What the police ever done for us, huh?

Someone come see me.

FREDDIE. What did they come see you for?

JAKE. My accounts. Start asking questions about the business.

FREDDIE. That's got nothing to do with me.

JAKE. Say the HMRC might do an audit. Check I been doing everything correctly. Declaring the right tax and that.

FREDDIE. Since when do the police care about audits?

JAKE. This guy wasn't police. Tax inspector he was. Says I could get in a lot of trouble if things don't add up. Could even go to prison for that. And when I ask what he means by *might* do an audit he says well, that depends on your brother Frederick.

FREDDIE. The slippery bitch.

I'll tell them. Tell them she's getting people to threaten you.

JAKE. You don't tell them a thing about me, Freddie.

I wonder if all this doughnut sugar's been going to your brain.

Didn't you get any with the sprinkles?

(*Bites one.*) Oh this one's got chocolate cream inside – here, you want it?

FREDDIE. You know most people, if they got an email like that. I dunno. They'd maybe email back or say something or I don't know but they sure as hell wouldn't be talking about doughnuts.

JAKE. Well, most people if you told them might not know you're full of shit. Most people don't know you like I know you.

FREDDIE. Maybe you don't know me, Jake.

JAKE. No? You know I actually laughed when I got your email. Like proper lols. I mean I knew you were one crazy motherfucker – but this, this. But then as I deleted it I thought actually it's no different to anything else in Freddie's little world, is it? When you shat yourself when you were seven it were the fault of the coach who didn't pause for a toilet break. When you failed every subject in Year 9 it were the fault of staff out to get you. And now, I don't know, you can't get laid and it's the fault of some teacher you banged a million years ago.

FREDDIE. I don't have to... justify myself to you. I remember, alright.

JAKE. Yeah? What do think you remember?

FREDDIE. I don't *think*... you know what, to hell with you, and her.

JAKE. Tell me. Go on.

I'm your brother and I should... I promise to listen. She invited you round her house and she...

FREDDIE. Yeah.

JAKE. Say it. You went round her house and she...

FREDDIE. Like I wrote in the email.

JAKE. No you didn't actually say it. You went round hers and she... it begins with an R.

Cos that's what you're saying, right? That you didn't want to and she

FREDDIE. I'm saying I wasn't old enough to make that decision. She bought me things and said things and so that I'd... do what she wanted.

JAKE. Poor Freddie.

FREDDIE. I don't care what you think, Jake.

JAKE. It's not what I think, Freddie. Cos what I think is if I hadn't grown up sharing baths with you then I'd properly doubt if you've even got a dick under there cos you're acting like a right pussy.

You think you can barely get a girl now; you'd be a fucking pariah if this got out.

FREDDIE. I know it's hard to believe, or to understand if you haven't... But I need people to know, whatever the consequences for me. So that she can't hurt someone else.

JAKE. And this hurt, this is a realisation that you've suddenly come to a million years later.

FREDDIE. Seven years.

Beat.

Don't you read the paper ever? Most people don't, at the time, but then later – like the footballer, or the. It's later when all these people remembered.

JAKE. I remember too. Do you know what I remember?

I remember innocent Freddie bragging about he could get away with anything at school cos he had this young eager teacher who'd follow after him like a loyal dog. That you bet you could get her number to prove it. That she was gagging for it and you could take her any time you wanted.

But you know what I remember more clearly, little brother. The night I caught you kissing my girlfriend. And walloped you.

FREDDIE. That wasn't the same night.

JAKE. And you said you didn't want some little frigid sixteen-year-old anyway when you could have a real woman, could have *her*. And I told you you were full of shit, like always.

FREDDIE. It wasn't – and it don't matter if it were, the point is –

JAKE. And you came back early in the morning, woke me up and stuck your fingers under my nose. *Now who's full of shit?* you said.

FREDDIE *hits a wall. Starts hitting it over and over like an angry toddler.*

Come on, Freddie.

FREDDIE. You don't believe me.

JAKE. Freddie.

FREDDIE. I know what happened to me. And you don't believe me.

JAKE. I believe you.

FREDDIE. You're just saying that.

He goes and holds him, stops him banging the wall. It's suddenly very tender.

JAKE. I believe you, Freddie. And I've got your back. Always had your back, haven't I.

He strokes his hair.

Come on, have a doughnut.

There's a good chocolate one you'll like.

Gives him the bitten one.

FREDDIE *laughs. Takes the doughnut.*

How I'd calm you when you were a kid too. Mum was worried you'd be diabetic.

FREDDIE. Say one of these is like three Big Macs.

JAKE. You could do with putting on some weight.

FREDDIE. You sound like Mum.

JAKE. Yeah well. Someone's gotta take care of you.

FREDDIE. So you'll support me. With the police.

JAKE. No.

FREDDIE. But you said…

JAKE. You're right about the footballer. And those politicians. But she's not a footballer, Freddie.

And neither are you.

Not gonna be in any papers. Not gonna make a difference to no one.

FREDDIE. I can't just

JAKE. Yes you can. You will. You've managed the last seven years.

FREDDIE. Jake.

JAKE. Some of these parts, lots of the parts, at least when we started, my guys got from different places. Unofficial places. Tax office start auditing me, my whole shop, everything I built up for us gonna be finished. Don't know who she knows or what you did but you pissed off the wrong person. So you go tell the police you made a mistake, then you go tell her you made a mistake. And you make this go away.

FREDDIE.... Don't know if I can do that, Jake.

JAKE. Yes you can.

Cos any taxman or police come by here, I gonna tell them I don't have a brother.

Your mum died, and your dad died, and you won't have a brother neither. You'll be an orphan, Freddie.

You think Dad gave it to *you* bad? I always made sure I took the worst. For you. I've always had your back, and I need to know you have mine.

Freddie?

Scene Five

The humanities office.

MARY *is alone in the office with* GEORGIA.

GEORGIA. Can I give a fake name?

MARY. I'm not entirely sure, Georgia.

GEORGIA. It's actually really personal, and I don't want someone like actually looking at my fanny and knowing my name, you get what I'm saying? Making all small talk, 'Georgia, how was your weekend?' as she like stickin' her gloved finger inside me, cos it's just really personal.

MARY. I don't think uh they'll necessarily need to uh –

GEORGIA. Or how was that science test, Georgia? My dentist is always doing that and it's like how am I meant to answer when your fingers are in my mouth and what test are you even talking 'bout cos it's been six months and am I supposed to actually remember, like did she put that in my chart, and I'm not having it.

MARY. So here's the card for the clinic.

GEORGIA. Maybe it's just that the wax was too hot cos it's like forty quid at Oasis Salon, and why am I gonna pay that when I can do it myself for a fiver from Boots.

MARY. I think it's best to talk about this with the nurse.

GEORGIA. But I like talking to you, miss. You understand, cos you're practically the same age.

MARY. We're not the same age.

GEORGIA. Not actually, but practically.

MARY. It's probably best you get to class now, Georgia.

GEORGIA. Mrs Andrews ain't even there. It's Mr Abramovich covering and we're basically colouring maps. And I'm actually really stressed about this red bump.

MARY. Georgia, after everything you went through in the autumn, it worries me that a fifteen-year-old feels the need to... wax their pubic hair.

GEORGIA. Well, I wasn't going to take a photo with it looking all Scary Spice.

MARY. Georgia, are you being serious?

GEORGIA. You're going all adult voice.

MARY. Why are you taking photos of yourself?

GEORGIA. Not for myself, for my boyfriend.

MARY. Georgia, did you not listen to any of that assembly we had last month?

GEORGIA. That copper was clueless. It's just foreplay. What's the difference if two people are in the same room naked or in separate rooms and see a photo of each other naked? More safe actually, can't get an STI.

MARY. Georgia.

GEORGIA. It's really not a big deal. The phone is just an extension of my sexuality.

MARY. Is that what your boyfriend told you?

GEORGIA. Don't be stupid, man.

MARY. So you're telling me it wasn't your boyfriend's idea?

GEORGIA. No it was his idea.

MARY. Well, that doesn't sound very healthy to me, that he's demanded that you –

GEORGIA. Honestly, you sound like my mum which is how come I never tell her anything. He didn't demand, he asked. He didn't like put a leash on me, walk me to Boots and then take me home and rip hairs off my fanny. I did that.

Do you have a boyfriend, miss?

MARY. We're not talking about me.

GEORGIA. A girlfriend?

MARY. Georgia.

GEORGIA. Cos you're wearing make-up. And nice clothes. And you got a fake tan. I'm not saying it looks bad, but like I can tell. And why do you do that? Probably it makes you feel attractive. Which actually when there's people killing themselves with self-esteem issues is probably a good place to be. So if this turns my boyfriend on, it makes me feel attractive. And why is that a bad thing?

Pause.

MARY. Well, you've given me lots to think about. As I tell my friends, I learn as much from my students as they do from me.

GEORGIA. Do you really say that, miss? Cos that's a bit.

MARY. How have things worked out with your friend?

GEORGIA. I don't know what you're talking about.

MARY. Your friend Portia.

GEORGIA. Like I actually have no idea what you're talking about, miss.

MARY. We gave them fake names, from your English text, so that you wouldn't have to say who they were. You were worried because she wouldn't let you meet her boyfriend – the one who was getting her alcohol and such? And your other friend – *Nerissa* – said she thought he was controlling Portia, and you were worried?

GEORGIA. Was I?

MARY. So it's all resolved itself, has it? I was actually a bit worried when I reflected on it later. For your friend Portia – with this older boyfriend.

GEORGIA. No, he's fifteen too.

MARY. Oh. Right. Well, that's.

GEORGIA. How do you know if someone loves you?

MARY. That's. A difficult question. I suppose they usually tell you.

GEORGIA. Besides words though I mean. Like when we were making those lists in form, people said they thought compromise was most important for a healthy relationship. So like if my boyfriend wants to download *Fast and Furious 7* but I want to download *Fifty Shades of Grey*, like one of us has to compromise cos that's what you do when you're in love?

MARY. Yes. And maybe you'll find that you're actually rather interested in car films.

GEORGIA. And maybe he'll realise he's actually like interested in like tying people up for sex.

MARY. I suppose it would work that way too, yes.

I think the point from form was people in relationships help us try new things. Which is healthy. For example, when I was a Girl Scout we went white-water rafting, and I didn't want to go, but my leader encouraged me to try it. And so I did. As it turns out I don't really like white-water rafting but I really wouldn't have known that if I hadn't been willing to try.

GEORGIA. Is that like a metaphor? The white-water rafting?

MARY. No. It was white-water rafting.

GEORGIA. Oh right. Just you being a Girl Scout isn't really about relationships.

Portia's boyfriend is all into like *Fifty Shades* kinda stuff, but I should just tell her it's like you said, right, miss, that it's good to try new things.

MARY. Well. Um.

GEORGIA. Or do you think it's like actually really dirty?

MARY. I haven't actually seen *Fifty Shades of Grey*. But I think that what people – including Portia – do in the privacy of their own home in their own relationship is no one's business but theirs. And as long as everyone's consenting and being safe then it's not for us to stigmatise or judge.

GEORGIA. That's like actually really helpful, miss.

MARY. I'm glad.

GEORGIA. What did you do in the Girl Scouts? Did you do camping and stuff?

MARY. Yes of course. Were you thinking about joining? I think it might be really good for you.

GEORGIA. No thanks. I just wondered if you could show me how to do a knot. For Portia? Cos she said last time they had to like cut the rope with scissors cos they did it too tight.

MARY. I'm not sure that's a good idea.

GEORGIA. How come? You said it was fine what she were doing.

MARY. I did say that, yes.

...

GEORGIA. It's cool, miss. I get it. Not really my problem anyhow. I'll just tell her to look on YouTube.

DIANE *enters*.

DIANE. Why aren't you in lesson?

GEORGIA. I thought I saw you in a meeting.

DIANE. And now you see me here. Telling you to go to lesson.

GEORGIA. I'm just talking to Miss Willis right now.

DIANE. No right now you're going to room 304 where Mr
Abramovich is waiting for you. And button up your shirt, I
can see your cleavage.

GEORGIA. You can't say that, miss.

DIANE. Do you mean I shouldn't say that? As it seems I *can*
since I just did.

GEORGIA. Miss, I can't help that I have big breasts. You can't
discriminate against me for that. The buttons don't do up,
there's nothing I can do.

DIANE. Yes, you can buy a bigger shirt. Goodbye, Georgia.

GEORGIA *sucks teeth, goes*.

MARY. Sorry, that was my fault. She's just been going through
a lot.

DIANE. She's running circles around you, you know that?

MARY. Maybe. But it's just I've made such progress with
Georgia. She's passing some of her tests even. But who
knows. Some of the stuff she was saying did make me a bit
worried, a bit uncomfortable.

DIANE. Did you tell her she was making you uncomfortable?

MARY. No because then she'll stop talking to me, and I think
I've built up a real trust with her. She's really just an
innocent girl who people perceive to be naughty so she plays
up to it, but it's all performance.

DIANE. Georgia Miles has many qualities but innocence is
certainly not one of them.

She knows you care, so she's exploiting that.

MARY. She's really just misunderstood.

DIANE. Don't say you haven't been warned. How's the new unit been going?

MARY. Well. We um started. I just wonder if it's really better to wait until Ms Rickards is back from sick leave.

DIANE. I've prepared all the materials for you.

MARY. Yes, but the students seemed to go off-script fairly quickly. It was barely two minutes in and one of the boys asked what felching was? And I don't know.

DIANE. Think of Sex and Relationships Education as a war zone and you're the journalist. Give the facts, show the photos, but don't get too close unless you want your head blown off.

MARY. So sex is a bomb?

DIANE. No, the students are. Over-wanked fuses and pornified nitroglycerine threatening to detonate at any moment, and trying to take you with them. Think of them as suicide bombers and you'll do just fine.

MARY. Diane. These children are

DIANE. That's your mistake, seeing them as children. Your Year 10 form. Connor Maguire was caught masturbating in the disabled loo over a photo of Judas from *Jesus Christ Superstar* that he'd stolen from the drama corridor; Lucy Matthews discovered one of Samuel Canning's pubes taped to her locker so responded by taping one of hers to his. They'll leave their arse-crack on show just to see what you'll say. They want to see you blush. They already know everything there is to know about sex. Most of them watched porn before they were out of nappies. They're going to have sex. Most of this lot already are. Don't try to change their minds. Just listen. Facilitate. They'll forget most of what you say when they leave the classroom anyway.

I should go relieve Mr Abramovich.

Oh, it means sucking out semen from a vagina or anus.

MARY. Excuse me?

DIANE. Felching. In case they ask you again. Let me know how it goes. (*Exits*.)

GEORGIA *reappears*.

GEORGIA. You alright, Miss Willis?

MARY. Georgia, why aren't you in class?

GEORGIA. It weren't your fault. Mrs Andrews has been a real cow these past few weeks.

MARY. Go to class, Georgia.

GEORGIA. Just wanted to say sorry. If I got you in trouble. I wouldn't want that. You're one of the alright ones, you know?

Beat. MARY *is moved/flattered*.

MARY. Go to class.

Georgia?

Tell your friend a Highwayman's Hitch. The knot comes out with one pull.

GEORGIA. Okay, miss.

Scene Six

Classroom. On the board it says 'CONSENT' in big letters.

BRANDON. But how do you know if a girl's consenting?

KAYLA. Oh my gosh, you are such a moron. Just go to sleep like Owen.

DIANE. It's a good. It's a good question.

KAYLA (*to* BRANDON). Cos she says yes, you idiot.

BRANDON. Yeah but you'd don't actually ask her, do you? You're supposed to say 'Can I have sex with you?'

RHYS. That's well gay.

NATHAN. Well, only if you're saying it to someone of the same sex.

RHYS. You got to be like seductive, put on the moves. It's not like a contract.

BRANDON. So how do you know?

AMANDA. Well, if they say no, which to be fair will probably happen a lot to you, then you know.

NATHAN. Can I just say that by saying how do we know if 'she' has consented that we're not being very inclusive.

RHYS. That's cos if a guy's having sex, then there's some pretty *rock-hard* evidence that he's consented.

NATHAN. Not necessarily.

RHYS. Yes necessarily. If I'm standing here with my hard-on. And I'm doing this. (*Starts thrusting.*) Oh look at me I'm not consenting. My hips are taking on a life of their own. I can't stop. (*Grabs hold of* LIAM*'s head, pretends to fuck it.*)

AMANDA. Leave him alone, Rhys.

RHYS. I'm saying if a guy had sex, then he consented.

NATHAN. That's sexist.

RHYS. *Women's Hour* is at it again.

NATHAN. If a girl wears a short skirt, is flirtatious, but then doesn't want sex, we – at least those of us who are not Neanderthals and are living in the current century – understand that of course those two things are compatible. That just because a girl *appears* to be up for sex based on what we're – perhaps unfairly – reading in to signifiers of her behaviour or what she wears – does not mean that she is consenting to sex.

KAYLA. Heya!

DESTINY. The prosecution rests, your honour!

NATHAN. So just because a guy seems to be up for sex, maybe he goes around the class with his erection pretending to hump other students and on the surface seems highly charged

and ready, in fact does not want to have sex at all; in all likelihood the highly sexualised performance is a cover for how unready he is for the real thing.

RHYS. Is he talkin' 'bout me?

DESTINY. The jury finds for the prosecution!

DESTINY *and* KAYLA *start singing/dancing in celebration.*

OWEN. Miss, can I say something?

KAYLA. Oh my gosh, is he awake?

OWEN. I had sex when I was fourteen. And like knowing me, probably everyone here would be like no surprise there. Because I would talk lots about sex and I knew lots of things because I watched a lot of porn and I have three older brothers. But actually I think it's like Nathan says. I wasn't ready. Even if on the outside it seemed like I was. And I wish, in truth, that I hadn't. I wish I was still a virgin.

I just wanted to say that.

Silence. Everyone's a bit stunned. Both that he's spoken at all, and by what he said.

Pause. He goes back to sleep.

DESTINY. Hands up, boys, if anyone else said they were ready when they actually weren't.

DIANE. We're not going to do that.

TAYLOR. According to *Cosmo*, sixty per cent of men think they weren't ready to have sex when they did.

DIANE. Please put your phone away.

DESTINY. We're doing a poll, hands up, boys.

DIANE. No, we're doing this lesson. We're. So we've established that saying no is not consenting. Any questions?

GRACE. Yeah but a girl doesn't have to say no, to not consent.

BRANDON. Well, then how do you know?

RHYS. Yeah? What do you mean they don't have to say no but it's still the same?

AMANDA. You can just tell sometimes that she's not in to it.

GRACE. Not being in to it isn't the same as not consenting. We've all had times we're not *that in to it* but for the sake of the other person.

LIAM. Have you felt that way with me?

GRACE. It was just... an example.

AMANDA. It's like grooming, right, the person doesn't say no necessarily but they're not consenting because they're not in a position to consent.

LIAM. You think sometimes I'm having sex with you and you're not *in to it*.

BRANDON. How do you decide if she's not in a position to consent?

GRACE. It wasn't you, per se.

RHYS. What does per se mean?

TAYLOR. If a guy is buying a girl gifts, offering advice or understanding, giving attention, using their reputation or taking her on holidays or trips. That's grooming.

NSPCC website.

DIANE. Can you put your phone away please?

TAYLOR. It's for educational purposes.

KAYLA. That's not grooming, that's just a relationship.

DESTINY. You best bet any man be buying me gifts and holidays, and giving me attention.

DIANE. I think we're getting slightly off-topic.

NATHAN. Can I just say again that by saying a guy buying a girl gifts we're not being very inclusive in this discussion.

KAYLA. There's a girl yeah, not saying who, but she's at this school and she gets a pack of cigarettes for each blow job she gives.

DIANE. This isn't a forum for speaking about other students.

KAYLA. I didn't say who it was.

DIANE. Especially not a place for spreading rumours.

KAYLA. It's true, swear down.

DIANE. Can we stick to the topic?

KAYLA. Cos if the throat herpes doesn't kill her the lung cancer will, you see what I'm saying?

DIANE. No, I don't. And I don't see what –

KAYLA. 'S called intersectionality that. When the herpes meets the lung cancer.

NATHAN. That's not what intersectionality is.

KAYLA. Shut up, man. You all think I'm making stuff up but it's true. Don't know why I bother.

RHYS. Miss, this is like proper worrying me now. Like how do you know if you're doing the groom thing. Like all them things Taylor just read out, like kinda what I do with my girlfriend. So how do I know if I'm like grooming her?

DIANE. You would know, alright. Now what we're talking about today

RHYS. Read 'em out again

TAYLOR. Buying a girl gifts.

DIANE. I'm leading this class, Taylor

TAYLOR. Offering advice

DIANE *takes phone off her.*

DIANE. I told you to put your phone away.

TAYLOR. Can I have it back, miss?

DIANE. No.

TAYLOR. That's my property.

DIANE. It's school property now.

TAYLOR. That's assault. You just assaulted me. Just came up and touched me. Not allowed to do that, miss.

KAYLA. It's true, miss.

Beat. They all watch her.

DIANE. Get out.

TAYLOR. What?

DIANE. Take your phone. And get out.

Everyone. Get out. Just go to class.

AMANDA. But the bell hasn't rung yet, miss.

DIANE. Did you not hear me? I am the teacher! I am... the adult here and I am telling you to leave.

The STUDENTS *all leave.* DIANE*'s alone.*

FREDDIE *appears at her classroom door eating a biscuit. He breaks the top off and licks the middle.*

But of course he's not there. He's in fact at her front door.

Scene Seven

Outside DIANE*'s house.*

FREDDIE *tosses the biscuit into a bush. Rings the bell.* PETE *answers the door.*

PETE. Yes?

Hello?

FREDDIE. I, uh... sorry, wrong house.

PETE. Who are you looking for?

FREDDIE. 'S alright, mate. Sorry to've. (*Goes to leave.*)

PETE. I know who you are.

Pause.

FREDDIE. Tell her I... I dropped the uh... the allegation. Tell her I stopped by and.

PETE. Why did you do it?

FREDDIE. Just leave it, mate.

PETE. I'm about to give my six-year-old daughter a bath. I just fed her her tea and I'm about to give her a bath.

I don't know how you got this address. But this is my home. This is our lives. You and your generation just think you can... and it scares me, the world I'm bringing up my daughter in. Where you just click, send, say without a second thought. Without thinking through the intention or the consequences.

FREDDIE. You can save your little speech for your daughter, mate.

PETE. I'm trying to help you.

FREDDIE. You know fuck-all about my life.

PETE. I know your parents are dead. I know your brother has shady business dealings. And I don't want you to –

FREDDIE. That's you, is it? Leave my brother be.

PETE. Diane obviously tried to help you once. And I'm just trying to do the same.

FREDDIE. Help me? *Help me?* Threatening my brother?

PETE. No one's. What he's doing, if he's doing things dishonestly, is no one's fault but his own, Freddie.

FREDDIE. Stop saying my name like you know me. You pretend you never heard my name or my brother's.

PETE. It's maybe too late for him, Freddie. But maybe not for you. And that's why I'm trying to give you advice, because I know that despite what you've done, for reasons that are difficult for me to fathom, Diane cares about you.

FREDDIE *spits. It lands at* PETE*'s feet.*

FREDDIE. Fuck your charity. You lay off my brother or I go back to the police, tell them what she done.

PETE. Your brother is responsible for his own actions.

FREDDIE. Won't just be your wife, yeah. Neighbourhood find out she's a paedo, people'll be egging your house, smashin' shit through your windows. Your daughter'll be scared to leave the house.

You pick up that phone right now, tell whoever you need to tell to leave my brother alone.

PETE. That's not how it works.

FREDDIE. Do it or I'll, right now. Detectives sitting by the phone just waiting for me to change my mind again.

PETE. Then you'll force me to look into your dad.

FREDDIE. You think I care? The bastard's dead.

PETE. And he hasn't submitted a tax return for the last decade. That rusty box you're living in, they'll take it. The TV, the fridge, the couch, your bed. Everything. I haven't brought it to anyone's attention because I don't want to make things any harder for you than they already are.

FREDDIE. You know where I'm from, we don't hide behind some fucking paper, we roll up our sleeves if we've got a problem.

PETE. Well. I have more dignity than that. And so should you. I have morals.

FREDDIE. You think your wife has morals? When she was moaning as she forced my head between her legs? Do you? When I was nibbling on that little birthmark she's got inside her thigh, the one that looks like a clover? She didn't even want me to wear a condom. Wanted to really make sure she could feel my teenage dick inside her, she said.

Your daughter's six, you said? Have a good hard look at her in the bath. Make sure she doesn't look like me.

All makes sense now. Dusty old suit-and-tie man provides the roof, and the supper, and the holidays to Center Parcs. But needs to get young boys to fulfil the part you can't get up to.

PETE. With the exception of people like my wife, people for the most part don't care about people like you. Because they see you for what you are. A burden.

Goodbye, Freddie. Don't say I didn't try to help you.

FREDDIE *spits in* PETE*'s face.*

FREDDIE. The DNA might help with the paternity test.

Scene Eight

PETE *and* DIANE*'s house. Night.*

PETE. Where've you been?

DIANE. Sorry. I didn't mean to worry you. (*Kisses him lightly on the lips.*)

PETE. Have you been drinking? Jesus, Diane.

DIANE. Relax, Pete, it's one night.

PETE. Who were you drinking with?

DIANE. Myself.

PETE. Your phone was off.

DIANE. I lost it with my students today and I just needed.

But I'm home now.

She goes to her laptop, opens it.

PETE. Why don't you leave that and come to bed?

DIANE. I've got schoolwork.

PETE. I've been waiting up for you all night. (*Touches her.*) Come on, Diane. Come upstairs.

DIANE (*pushes his arm off*). I'm not in the mood, Pete.

PETE. No, you're only in the mood for your laptop, right?

You know I thought if I could be more like, if I could – so I…

But I can't, can I, Diane?

SluttyMILFs, NaughtyMoms, DicksinDetention.com

Is that what turns you on? Some skaterboy giving some woman anal over a kitchen counter instead of. You'd rather that than...

DIANE. Than what?

PETE. Than me?

DIANE. You fucking feel threatened by some stupid video on the internet?

PETE. Don't you swear at me.

DIANE. You're being ridiculous.

PETE. Am I?

DIANE. Look at me, I'm a whale. I'm sorry if carrying a two-tonne sack in my stomach doesn't exactly put me in the mood.

PETE. But that doesn't put you off some kid with a twelve-inch cock cumming in some mother's hair!

DIANE. Maybe it makes me feel desired! Maybe it's the idea, however fake, however staged, that despite my stretch marks and an arse that's gone saggy, some young stud might still want to just take me and have his way with me. What's wrong with that? Tell me you don't fantasise about some younger girl, younger than me

PETE. Did you have sex with him?

Pause.

DIANE. No.

Pause.

PETE. He came here today. To the house.

He dropped the allegation.

DIANE. That's... that's good news, that's a relief. I'm so relieved.

How come he's dropping it?

PETE. Because it's a lie, right?

DIANE. Yes. But. Why has he decided?

PETE. Perhaps he came to his senses.

DIANE. Is that what he said?

PETE. I shut down his brother's business. And told him his house would be next.

DIANE. You what? Are you serious?

PETE. Yes.

DIANE. What did you do that for?

PETE. You told me to take care of it.

DIANE. I didn't tell you to – what does his brother have to do with this? I don't even know his brother.

PETE. I fixed it didn't I?

DIANE. And his house? Christ, Pete.

PETE. You told me to.

DIANE. I told you to – I didn't mean –

PETE. Why are you protecting him?

DIANE. I'm not.

PETE. I thought you'd be happy.

DIANE. I... am.

I'm sorry. It's the pregnancy. It's making me...

Why are we even fighting?

PETE. How did he know about your birthmark?

DIANE. What?

He suddenly puts his hand on her inner thigh.

PETE. That one. He described it.

I put my job on the line to make this go away.

Pause. She moves away from him.

DIANE. I didn't have sex with him.

I let him touch me though.

PETE. When was this?

DIANE. I don't remember exactly.

PETE. Diane.

DIANE. You and I had gone on a few dates by then.

He cries silently.

I didn't say the other day because I didn't want to hurt you.

Pause. PETE *wipes tears away.*

Will you please say something?

PETE. And the other stuff? The... I can't even –

How do you know you weren't... that the reason you helped him and...

Did you want to? Were you attracted to him?

When you mentioned him the other day, I was picturing this man. This wrestler or something. And then he came and he was, even seven years on. A kid. He just looked like this feral lost kid.

He spat in my face.

DIANE. What?

PETE. He spat on the porch. And then he spat in my face.

DIANE. Oh my god. What did you do?

PETE. I said goodbye and I shut the door.

DIANE. You didn't...?

PETE. What?

DIANE. I don't know.

PETE. What?

DIANE. I don't know. You just let him spit on you.

PETE. I didn't let him.

DIANE. You let him get away with that.

PETE. What was I supposed to do?

DIANE. I don't know. Spit back. Hit him or something?

PETE. Is that what you would have wanted?

DIANE. It sounds like he deserved it.

PETE. Messed him up a bit. Showed him what's what. Left him with something to show for it. That what I should have done?

DIANE. He spat in your face. So yes.

PETE. And then I'd be just like him. Is that what you would like?

DIANE. I just don't want him to think that you're soft and he can do what he wants.

PETE. Is that what *you* think?

DIANE. I just want to make sure everything's alright.

PETE. You asked me to take care of things and I did.

DIANE. Fine. Yes. Sorry. I'm exhausted. We're both exhausted. Let's not – Pete?

She goes to him. Hugs him. They stand there hugging for a long time.

Then there's a shift.

And he begins kissing her. Begins to undo her blouse.

Pete.

He takes off his shirt. Begins savagely pulling at her clothes. Kissing her body.

Pete, not tonight.

He takes off his belt.

Pete.

He pushes her down. With her pregnant belly she can't move very well.

Pete!

PETE. That's what you said you wanted, isn't it? For someone to just take you and have their way with you.

DIANE. Stop it, Pete.

PETE. It's what you said.

DIANE. Pete, enough.

He's been continually removing his clothes, and removing some of hers.

PETE. The kind of guy who messes someone up.

DIANE. Get off me, Pete. I can't move.

I said get off of me!

She manages to get him off, breaking something in the process.

PETE. Or is it only fifteen-year-old dick you like doing this to you.

She slaps him.

Both of them are breathless. Sit/lean against furniture.

The phone rings. PETE *exits. But the phone continues ringing. No one answers it.*

Scene Nine

A bar.

MARY*'s sat with an empty bottle of wine, and very little remaining in the wine glass in front of her. She spots* DIANE *enter the bar.*

MARY. Diane! Diane!

DIANE. I see you. You can stop waving.

MARY. Oh god, Diane.

DIANE. Did you drink all of this?

MARY. Is it bad? Of course it's bad. Oh god. What did they say to you?

DIANE. They're going to call you. Ask you to come in tomorrow.

MARY. Will she be there?

DIANE. No, of course she won't be there.

MARY. God, so when do I get to see her?

DIANE. You don't, Mary.

MARY. No. Is she alright?

DIANE. None of us has seen her, Mary.

MARY. And what will happen to him?

DIANE. That's a police matter. Tomorrow is just about the internal investigation, about you. To determine if there's been professional misconduct.

MARY. Yes. Okay. Oh god, Diane. Oh god, you know?

DIANE. I do yes.

MARY. So what did she say?

DIANE. She wasn't there, Mary. It was just me, the Head, and the Chair of the Governors.

MARY. Do you want some wine? Oh no you're –

So what did they say? They've told me so little. Just the, you know, the crux of things.

DIANE. I don't know that I can really say, Mary. That's what tomorrow's for.

I shouldn't even really be here.

MARY. Oh god, what's going to happen to her?

DIANE. Did you really not know, Mary? What he was doing to her?

MARY. She said her friend, her friend – Portia.

DIANE. *I need advice. So I have this friend...* And it never occurred to you it was actually Georgia talking about herself? That she was Portia?

MARY. When you say it like that, it sounds, it sounds obvious, but it wasn't. The way she. Oh god, Diane.

DIANE. Even if you thought it was her friend, you didn't think to report it?

MARY. She said the boyfriend was fifteen.

DIANE. He was.

MARY. And I just never thought, if he was the same age, that it could be that he could be...

DIANE. Abusing her?

MARY. Oh god, please don't use that word, is that what they're, is that what she's saying he was doing?

DIANE. From what I gather Georgia is still protecting him, says he loves her.

MARY. I could've helped. But I didn't know, Diane.

DIANE. I shouldn't be doing this, Mary, but you should know, for tomorrow. It's not just about not reporting. It's about. Did they tell you how her mother found out? About their relationship?

MARY. They said there was a diary. Her mother looked through her diary.

DIANE. That was after.

> She came home, went into her daughter's bedroom in the basement.

> Georgia was tied up to the bedposts. Naked.

> There were used condoms on the floor. Multiple used condoms.

> And when Mum asked her what had happened, all she would say was: the knots were meant to undo really easily. Ms Willis said they would.

MARY. I think I'm going to throw up.

DIANE. Part of the thrill was leaving her there, used. So she told him she'd be able to undo them herself after.

> When she wouldn't tell Mum what happened, Mum took her laptop.

MARY. Oh god.

DIANE. There was a folder, like a diary where she'd write emails to herself. He loved her. He loved her so much which was why he bought her all the alcohol and pot she wanted.

> Georgia wasn't as unstudious as we all thought. Her e-diary had footnotes. Mum printed off the emails for the Head. (*Pulls out a copy.*)

> 'He wants to share me with his friends. To show me off. I don't really like it, but people in relationships help us try new things. And love is all about compromise. And we shouldn't stigmatise people who like to tie people up for sex. It's healthy.'

> Footnote. Ms Willis.

MARY. I didn't, I didn't. Oh god, I did. But she's. I didn't mean. Oh god.

> At least they used condoms. I mean that's something. Oh god, what a thing to say.

> She just seemed so... okay. The way she talked about taking photos of herself, like she was mature. And I was the

immature one. The way she described it, she made it seem all so... consensual.

DIANE. I guess she thought it was.

MARY. She was starting to behave in her classes and I just wanted to... save her. Oh god.

DIANE. You'll get through this.

MARY. You can just breeze through, not let them effect you.

She wasn't just a student to me. I didn't just fail some student.

It's Georgia. It's like I failed my friend.

Which I know sounds crazy.

DIANE. It doesn't sound crazy

MARY. It sounds crazy. You shouldn't care about students, not like that.

Not thinking like they're your friend. Not like them like that. And she liked me. And I liked that she liked me. I'm a crazy person.

DIANE. No you're not.

MARY. I am. Like right now, right now all I can think about is that I'll never get to see her again. You don't understand, Diane.

DIANE. I slept with a student.

Years ago.

So I understand, Mary.

I understand that to truly care you have to like them. And if you like them then where is the line? The teachers the students remember fondly are always the ones who were also a bit like their friends. Where the line was a bit blurred. Where they took the time to care.

We're alike, Mary. I understand. So trust me when I say you'll be okay.

MARY.... You did what?

MARY*'s mobile goes.*

DIANE. That's probably the Head.

Stands. Pulls some aspirin out of her purse.

Drink lots of water.

Exits.

MARY (*answering phone*). Hello?

Scene Ten

Classroom.

Like at the start, the STUDENTS *are not seated as they're teacherless.*

RHYS. I heard she were like tied up covered in five guys' spunk and her mum walks in, no lie.

DESTINY. Nasty.

BRANDON. What a slut.

KAYLA. Can I just say I was telling you 'bout what a skank she were ages ago, sleeping with guys for ciggies like a low-class prozzy and no one listened to me.

DESTINY (*sings*). 'Sitcks and stones may break my bones but chains and whips excite me.'

A few of them start dancing, singing.

MR ABRAMOVICH *enters.*

MR ABRAMOVICH. Take your seats.

KAYLA. Oh my days you must be joking me.

DESTINY. Mr Abramovich, why you here?

BRANDON. Where's Mrs Andrews? She have the baby?

MR ABRAMOVICH. Umm… I believe you have a recently finished a unit on healthy relationships.

KAYLA. Actually I was just telling everyone 'bout this girl which is really pertinent

TAYLOR. I don't think we finished the unit actually, cos miss went all –

MR ABRAMOVICH. Well, we're umm… moving on. For the next six weeks we'll be looking at interview skills. So if everyone could sit down, and I'd like you to write down a job you'd like to do. When you're an adult.

Scene Eleven

Outside FREDDIE*'s flat.*

FREDDIE *has just arrived, holding a couple of bags of food from a newsagent's.*

He stops when he realises DIANE *is standing at the front of his home.*

They look at each other. Pause.

DIANE. I don't know how I got here.

I mean I walked but. I didn't walk with the intention of arriving here. Did I come here before? I must have. But why? To drop off some missing work or – don't answer that. It doesn't matter.

There's this student at school, Georgia, and she…

I lost my job. Today.

Because of you. Well, because of. Actually I'm technically suspended but I'll resign before they fire me. One of my colleagues reported me to the Board of Governors. The woman I was mentoring actually. Because that's what happens. The mentee, the student – they all grow up and have minds of their own. And everything you taught them they use against you. I guess it's my fault. I told her what happened.

What did happen?

Freddie?

Because every time I.

There's the way I remember things. The way I want to remember things. And the way things happened. And I don't think I can tell them apart.

And maybe neither can you.

The only thing I can absolutely remember is the first time I saw you. You'd come into the office with your tie loose and askew, your shirt untucked, and a pen in your mouth, drawings on your hands, and you said – 'I think we're gonna be stuck together for a while. I apologise in advance.' And you smiled.

And I thought right then – or maybe it was later, maybe it's in hindsight that I thought what I think I thought then. I thought: 'If I were fifteen.'

So maybe I deserve all this. Because at the very least I thought it.

And when you'd come see me I liked it. I liked that you needed me.

Do you still smoke? Can I have a cigarette?

For a long time I hated you. I still hate you I think.

You knew what you were doing. Irrespective of me.

But.

I once confronted a man on the street because he threw some rubbish on the ground. I was honestly gobsmacked. And his response was: 'So what? What difference will my one piece of litter do? The world is collapsing with or without me picking up that piece of litter.'

Whether or not you knew what you were doing, I... (*Starts crying.*)

I... I need to...

I'm sorry.

I'm so very sorry...

She's hysterical now.

I'm so very sorry. I'm sorry, I'm sorry, I'm...

FREDDIE. Diane.

DIANE. No I don't want you to say anything. I didn't come here to

FREDDIE. Diane. You're bleeding.

She looks down. Touches between her legs. Heavy bleeding.

She slumps down.

Sound seems to go so that even the mouth of FREDDIE *asking her if she's okay has no sound.*

He pulls out his phone, dials 999.

The STUDENTS *watching move in closer.*

'Under Pressure' by Queen, featuring David Bowie begins to play.

End of Part One.

PART TWO: BEFORE

Scene Twelve

Middle of the night.

A ground-floor flat. Open-plan kitchen/living room. A sliding glass door leads to a small garden. Off the living room is the front door.

There are a few stairs, or a hallway, or another door that lead to a bedroom off.

It's raining heavily outside.

DIANE *enters through the front door, on the phone. Dressed from a night out. And drunk. She is twenty-two.*

DIANE. I'm in. No need to ring the rape police. Don't think
they come out when it's raining anyhow. Hold on. Just hold
on, my shoes. (*Takes off heels.*) What? I told you to hold on...
Oh, why what route is he taking you?... Tell him you're not
paying since he's taking the longer route, yeah tell him...
(*Takes out two aspirin and water.*) Yeah I heard, tell him it's a
free country. I mean, no, tell him tell him, it's not a free
country and you can't afford to pay for circuit routes,
circumspect, circumcised... (*Laughs.*) No don't ask him!
Don't ask him! Ask him!... what did he say?... (*Notices a
shot glass with Jack Daniels in it. Abandons the water/aspirin
and swigs the shot instead. And remembers word.*) Circuitous!
Are you home yet?... Text him to say what?... It's two in the
morning... He has to get up early. I don't know. To do taxes
or something... (*Laughs.*) God what am I doing with him? I
should just, but he's sweet. I don't know...

Just get out of the car. You can walk from there. He is properly
taking the piss, how did I get home before you. Just walk from
there. And don't pay. It's your human right... Just walk... it's
not raining that hard, think it's stopping. It's practically –

She flicks on the garden light. Standing on the other side of the glass door is a fifteen-year-old boy. FREDDIE.

DIANE *jumps in fright.*

Jesus Christ!

...

I just. I need to call you back. (*Hangs up.*)

She unlocks door, slides it open. FREDDIE is soaked in just a T-shirt and jeans. He's got a bloody nose, and some of the blood is on his shirt.

FREDDIE. You alright, miss? Did I give ya a fright?

DIANE. Freddie, what are you

When did you

What are you doing? It's two in the morning.

FREDDIE. Yeah, you was out late. Did you have a nice time?

DIANE. What's happened, Freddie?

FREDDIE. You wasn't answering your phone. So I just thought. And then you wasn't answering the door neither so just thought I'd. Wait.

Beat.

Her phone rings. Takes her some effort to focus and to figure out how to silence it.

You alright, miss?

DIANE. How did you know I lived here? How did you

Your – Christ – Freddie, your face.

Pause. They watch each other across the line of the door. It continues to rain on FREDDIE. A choice. They both know it.

DIANE. You'll get sick if you stand there like that. Get inside.

He enters.

FREDDIE. Don't want to ruin your evening or nothing. Shit, I'm getting mud all over your floor.

He struggles to take his shoes off, having to hop slightly, before eventually settling on sitting down on the floor to do it. He's still not totally at one with his body. She watches, her mind a million places.

You got any paper towel or something? I can wipe that up.

DIANE. It's fine.

FREDDIE. You got a nice place. Lived here long, miss?

DIANE. Freddie.

FREDDIE. My dad. He just.

DIANE. Did you call the police?

FREDDIE. I called you.

DIANE. You need to call the police.

FREDDIE. No thanks, miss.

DIANE. Freddie

FREDDIE. Will be fine in the morning. Just needed to not be in the house. He'll pass out soon though. It's fine, miss.

Who are you calling?

I'm not talking to no police.

DIANE. I'm not calling the police.

As the phone rings, she takes the aspirin and the water. Splashes water on her face to try to sober up. Voicemail.

Hi, Suzanne, sorry to call so late, it's Diane Williams, could you please ring me as soon as you get this, it's important, thanks.

FREDDIE. Who's Suzanne?

DIANE. Mrs Fitzgerald.

FREDDIE. What you ringing her for?

Beat. They watch each other.

The phone rings. DIANE *answers it before it's even completed a ring.*

DIANE. Hello... oh, Gemma... I just, sorry, I had to, did you get home okay?... Just tell him, sorry, listen, I just, I have to uh, I might actually vom, think I had a bit too much, send me a text when you get home... bye, bye.

FREDDIE. You drunk, miss?

DIANE.... No.

FREDDIE. Don't bother me, miss. 'S Saturday night. Allowed innit. Even for teachers.

DIANE. I'm not

FREDDIE. A teacher. I know. Pastoral assistant, teacher, same thing.

DIANE. Drunk. I'm not drunk.

FREDDIE. Can I have some squash?

DIANE. What?

FREDDIE. I'm thirsty.

DIANE. Sure.

She fixes some squash.

Do you want to – I don't know how much you want?

He downs a pint.

Notices shot glasses.

FREDDIE. Big night, huh?

DIANE. You shouldn't really be here, Freddie. And I. I don't know what

Why did you come here?

FREDDIE. Said to ring if I ever, in like an emergency you said, so I

And you weren't answering cos you were out with your boyfriend or whatever and so

DIANE. I wasn't out with my, how did you know where I lived?

FREDDIE. Saw you one time. Was on the bus and out the window saw you come in here.

Sorry. I'll go. I just thought. I'll go.

DIANE. Where are you going to go?

FREDDIE. Don't matter. I'll just wander for a couple hours and then go home.

DIANE. Freddie, it's two in the morning

FREDDIE *starts to put shoes on.*

FREDDIE. I can see it was stupid of me. Seemed like a good, maybe just crash here or, seemed like a good idea but can see you really don't want me here.

DIANE. No, Freddie.

FREDDIE. Just cos when you said if I needed anything or if he – but can see you didn't really, always doing stuff like that, not really understanding like true meanings, always a bit thick like that.

DIANE. You're not, Freddie, take your shoes off.

FREDDIE. You didn't mean it.

DIANE. I did. I do mean it. If you need anything then, yes

FREDDIE. Why didn't you answer your phone then?

DIANE. I was out. I didn't hear it.

FREDDIE. You don't want me here.

DIANE. I do. Please just stay and we'll figure this out. I won't be able to rest easy if you're wandering the streets. Please.

Beat.

FREDDIE. Why didn't you ring me back though?

DIANE. I... I was out, I didn't even know you called.

FREDDIE. Oh. Right. (*Almost takes his shoes off.*)

Can I use your phone?

DIANE. My phone?

FREDDIE. Mine's dead. Should probably ring my brother. He'll be worried.

DIANE. Good idea.

Hands phone. Beat.

FREDDIE. But you did know. See. There's your missed-call list. And it's not showing a little number at the bottom, so that means you've already seen it. The missed calls.

He puts her phone down. Goes to leave. She's forced to block his path.

DIANE. Freddie, you can't go out there. I'm sorry that I didn't – I was going to ring you tomorrow. I didn't realise it was, it was important. And I've. As you can see I've had something to drink and thought would be better to ring you when I was more fresh-faced tomorrow.

FREDDIE. Really?

DIANE. Yes. Really.

FREDDIE. You weren't ignoring me.

DIANE. No.

Now let's get some ice on that.

FREDDIE. No, it's alright. Looks worse than it is.

DIANE. Do you want to tell me what happened. Freddie?

FREDDIE. Not really. Do you want me to?

Cos if you want me to, I will. I'll do what you ask me to.

DIANE. Like at school, it stays confidential. Nothing leaves this flat, Freddie.

FREDDIE. Nothing happened. Nothing new anyhow. Was pissed. Started egging me on you know. Cos Charlie broke up with me. How I probably wasn't man enough for her, girl like that needs a real man. So I told him, told him – and I tried to ignore him, like you told me, like you told me I should, but I was so – so I asked him, yeah, what like him? A real man like him? And course he nods and laughs. I'd a shown her what's what he says. So I said, I told him if being a man like him's what it takes, then I'd rather not. I'd rather be the so-called pussy I am than a cunt like him. So that's when he...

DIANE. And then you came straight here?

FREDDIE. No, first I... I punched him back.

I know. I know, I shouldn't have.

But I just...

Am I gonna get in trouble now?

Do you think less of me?

You do.

DIANE. No.

No. I think. Truthfully. He had it coming.

I'm not, I'm definitely not advocating violence or, but

You stood up for yourself. That's. Good for you, Freddie.

I still think. The best thing would still be to go to the police.

FREDDIE. He got in a pub fight last year, so they stuck him in a cell, took almost two days to sober him up and let him go. But they put us in temporary care. Some foster lady, smelled like cat piss. Kept calling me buddy.

Not yet sixteen, miss. So that's what they'd do with me probably. Three months with some lady smells like cat piss. Better the bastard you know.

Three months, then I'm sixteen and I'm out.

Maybe I can move in here. That was a joke, miss.

DIANE. I know.

FREDDIE. Cos you had this look like. Sure your boyfriend wouldn't like it if I moved in here either.

DIANE. I.

I don't have a boyfriend actually.

FREDDIE. No? How come, miss?

DIANE. You must be freezing. I'll get you a towel, and some clothes. There's some cloths under the sink so you can clean your face. (*Exits to a room off.*)

FREDDIE *takes off his shoes.*

He takes off his wet jeans, finds something to drape them over.

Takes off his T-shirt. Wrings it out over the sink and hangs it somewhere.

He takes one of the used glasses. Pours a Jack Daniels.

At the same time:

(*Off.*) The hot water takes a few seconds to come on, well, more than, more like more like forty-five seconds so just gotta keep at it, or you can boil the kettle. But I usually just wait it out. The landlord keeps saying there's nothing he can do, 'can't control the weather, pipes get cold' but it's nothing to do with the, it shouldn't really take forty-five seconds to get some hot water, which actually is rather lukewarm. I only did laundry this morning so none of that's dry, so trying to find, I usually turn the heat off when I go out. Are you cold? I can turn on the heat, I only just got in so I haven't – it's just by the sink, the boiler, there's a little – I can do it in a second.

DIANE *enters with a pink hoodie and matching sweatpants.*

Sorry, it's the only thing I thought would be big enough.

(*Seeing him.*) Sorry, I didn't –

What are you drinking?

FREDDIE. Calms my nerves. Is that alright? (*Sips before she can answer.*)

Sorry. I shouldn't just take your stuff without asking. Sorry, miss, are you angry?

DIANE. No.

I'll um, put these here.

She goes to exit.

Heat.

Goes quickly to boiler, turns on heat, without looking at
FREDDIE *who is standing a foot away by the sink, then exits*
again to the bedroom.

He dries himself off with the towel. Slides off his wet
underwear and puts on the sweatpants.

Hangs the wet underwear on a kitchen-cupboard handle.

You decent?

FREDDIE. You're alright.

She re-enters. Averts gaze from his bare torso.

DIANE. I'm going to make some coffee. Would you like some?

FREDDIE. No you're alright, miss.

DIANE. Aren't you chilly?

He puts on the sweatshirt, she makes coffee. Tries not to
make an issue of the fact she has to touch his underwear to
open the cupboard. Checks her phone. Frustratingly, no
one's rung back.

FREDDIE. Do I look a bit gay, miss?

DIANE. It's all I had. I decided to go all fairtrade, clothing
where they actually – but quickly I realised that you can't
really shop *anywhere* and by then I'd thrown out most of my
clothes, well, donated, so.

FREDDIE. But I mean do you reckon if I was to walk down the
street like this people'd think I was gay?

DIANE. There's nothing wrong with being gay.

FREDDIE. Do you think I'm gay?

DIANE. A person's sexuality is their business.

FREDDIE. Do you think my sexuality is gay?

DIANE. No.

FREDDIE. Even if you met me wearing this?

DIANE. A pink suit wouldn't make you gay.

FREDDIE. No, but would you *think* I was gay?

DIANE. No.

FREDDIE. Even dressed like this?

DIANE. Yes even dressed like that.

FREDDIE. How do you know I'm straight though?

DIANE. You've talked about your girlfriend.

FREDDIE. But like the first time you met me, did you know my sexuality?

DIANE. Yes.

FREDDIE. Did you? How?

DIANE. I don't know. I just… knew.

The kettle goes, she turns away.

FREDDIE. You alright, miss?

You're not like

Standing still.

You should eat something. Sober you up quicker than coffee.

Trust me.

Think I saw in your

Goes to cupboard where squash was and pulls out some biscuits. The kind with cream layer in the middle.

Takes one for himself. Holds packet to her.

Go on.

She takes one. Holds it.

DIANE. Why weren't you at your exam yesterday?

FREDDIE. I was.

DIANE. Freddie, you're in my flat. In the middle of the night. Eating my biscuits. You could at least do me the decency of telling me the truth.

FREDDIE. I weren't in the mindset.

I can resit.

DIANE. You should've come to me before. Before you didn't sit it.

FREDDIE. How'd you know I weren't there?

DIANE. I have eyes.

FREDDIE. But you weren't moderating the exam.

Were you looking for me, miss? Checking up on me?

Beat.

That's nice, miss. Well nice that you noticed. Sorry I lied.

DIANE. I care about you, Freddie. I'm trying to help.

FREDDIE. It was just the break-up with Charlie. Complicated innit? Messed with my head innit?

DIANE. You should have come to me.

FREDDIE. Yeah, it's just, it was sort of about you and that.

DIANE. What does it have to do with me?

FREDDIE. Can I have some more JD?

I just still feel really wound up.

He pours one, downs it, pours another, and also one for her. Hands it to her before she can object.

Charlie asked me about the bracelet. (*Holds up a string bracelet around his wrist.*)

DIANE. And you told her I gave it to you.

FREDDIE. No. And that was part of it. Tried to make like I bought it but then she were asking lots of questions like where I bought it from, knew I was lying, so started accusing me of cheating on her with someone else.

DIANE. Why didn't you just tell her I gave it to you?

FREDDIE. Dunno.

Just thought. Like it's *our thing*, you know?

Like I'd have to explain how you said your mum used to make you a bracelet as a good-luck charm to help you focus, and that's why you – but I'd be like telling your personal stuff about your family.

DIANE. If that's why she broke up with you, then tell her. I don't mind. Really.

FREDDIE. But I don't want to. I like that it's this thing that just you and I know. The bracelet. Something you gave specially for me. And it's kinda more special if it's a secret.

You said that didn't you, about the bracelet being a secret.

DIANE. I don't think that's exactly what I said. It's like, what it means to you, the fact that it's good luck or meaningful or reminds you that you can do things or whatever it is you make it mean, then that's, that's the secret I guess, but the bracelet itself is not...

Now I'm confusing myself.

FREDDIE. No one ever gave me nothing before. Charlie never did. Always said it was for the boy to buy the girl stuff. And she'd always be on at me. Got a spray tan for her one time. Joined a gym for her. And she'd still be on at me like was I going and was I seeing results. Like I weren't buff enough, like I had a shit body compared to other guys she could be with, you know?

DIANE. You don't have a shit body.

FREDDIE. Do you think?

DIANE. Anyway most girls will be interested in your... thoughtful personality.

FREDDIE. Shit, that's totally code for I have a shit body.

DIANE. No.

FREDDIE. That I'm bare ugly. 'But he's thoughtful.'

DIANE. Freddie, no. You've got a very nice I was just trying to say that that's not all that you have.

FREDDIE. Thanks, miss.

DIANE. And I think. Truthfully. That you're better off without Charlie. That you might concentrate better on your studies, on your life.

FREDDIE. Guess I'm just worried that after Charlie, even though I'm better off, no one would ever fancy me.

DIANE. They will. There will be lots of girls that will fancy you. That I'm sure do.

She bites into her cookie.

FREDDIE. Do you fancy me, miss?

That was a joke.

What you doing? You can't do it like that. You gotta lick the middle out first.

DIANE. But then you don't get the biscuit with the cream.

FREDDIE. Yeah but then you don't get the sugar high. And it don't last as long.

He takes the top off his cookie. Starts licking the centre. She watches.

As a kid could make it last an hour. One biscuit. Cos knew I'd be sad when it was over. Just gotta go really slowly.

Go on.

DIANE. I'm alright.

FREDDIE. You have to. Killing me knowing you ate it like that.

She laughs. Takes another. They're both licking the middle.

DIANE. I feel stupid. I feel like I'm eight.

FREDDIE. Good to feel like a kid sometimes.

Beat. She drinks her Jack Daniels.

DIANE. You never called your brother. Don't you think you should call him? Tell him you're here?

FREDDIE *has noticed her CD collection.*

FREDDIE. Hold up. You have CDs? No one buys CDs any more.

Flips through them. Stops on one.

Holy shit. 'Under Pressure'? Can't believe you have this. It's like my favourite song.

DIANE. How old *are* you?

FREDDIE. My mum used to sing this to me.

DIANE. Your mum?

FREDDIE. We'd jump around to it together with our eyes closed.

DIANE. Queen fan, huh?

FREDDIE. More just Freddie Mercury fan. Why she named me Freddie?

DIANE. Seriously?

FREDDIE. This song. Him and David Bowie singing. David's my middle name.

DIANE. Freddie David.

Our mums must've been alike. Named me after her favourite singer too.

FREDDIE. Diana Ross or something?

DIANE. I wish. John Mellancamp.

FREDDIE. Your real name's John?

DIANE. No. She named my brother Jack.

Jack and Diane?

(*Sings*.) 'A little ditty about Jack and Diane.
Two American kids growin' up in the heartland.'

FREDDIE. You American?

DIANE. No. She just liked the song.

(*Sings*) 'Oh yeah life goes on. Long after the thrill of living is gone.'

Bit weird really. Brother and sister. Specially since the first verse is Jack fingering Diane.

(*Laughs*.) Sorry. Ignore me.

FREDDIE. Do you miss her?

DIANE....

Every day.

FREDDIE. Me too.

Not like, not your mum. I didn't know your mum.

I meant

DIANE. I know what you meant.

FREDDIE. She why you work with fuck-ups like me?

DIANE. Freddie.

FREDDIE. I'm only joking, miss. But it was her, right? You told me she was a teacher.

DIANE. Yeah.

FREDDIE. She'd be proud of you. You're a good person, miss. Diane. You're a good person.

Dunno, you like properly care. Do all this small stuff with your organic clothing, and volunteering and helping kids like me.

DIANE. You make me sound like – it's just small things. It's nothing. Tiny imprints.

FREDDIE. But all them tiny imprints eventually make a dent. What your mum said, right?

DIANE. You remembered that.

FREDDIE. Course. I remember everything you say.

You know what the first thing I thought when I decided not to turn up to the exam? How I'd disappoint you.

You're better than our school, miss. Better than kids like me.

DIANE. Freddie, if you only knew what – how much potential you have. And I know people throw that around, and it's a cliché, but if you just applied yourself. If you only saw in you what I see in you.

FREDDIE. Do I turn out alright, Diane? In the future? I try to see past school, and my dad, to when I'm like you, twenty-one

DIANE. Twenty-two

FREDDIE. Twenty-two, and I can't see it. Do it turn out alright?

DIANE. Yes.

Pause.

Let's make this bed for you.

Goes to start to make the couch into a pull-out bed.

FREDDIE. It's fine. I can just sleep on it like this.

DIANE. You sure?

FREDDIE. Yeah, slept on couches plenty of times.

DIANE. Here's some blankets.

He takes off the hoodie. Stands in just the sweatpants.

I can see if I have some pyjamas.

FREDDIE. I'm alright.

DIANE. Sure.

FREDDIE. Why didn't you tell your friend I was here?

When she rang earlier?

Pause.

He holds the hoodie to his face.

Smells like you.

With a hint of me now.

Beat.

When I wank off I think about you sometimes.

Most times.

But can never quite conjure the smell.

DIANE. Freddie.

FREDDIE. Diane.

He kisses her. She pulls away.

DIANE. I'm sorry if I gave you the wrong idea.

FREDDIE. Right.

Right.

Fuck.

Shit.

I'm always. Always.

Feel like a right twat now.

DIANE. You shouldn't.

FREDDIE. Stupid. Stupid to think you'd actually, fit like you, nice like you, would actually

DIANE. Where are you going?

FREDDIE *gets his wet T-shirt. Puts it on.*

Freddie, don't overreact.

FREDDIE. Just a pussy like my dad said, why would you

DIANE. Freddie, would you stop it

FREDDIE. I'm so embarrassed.

I thought you

So stupid

I actually thought you

DIANE. I do! I do alright.

I…

Fuck.

I look at you and I…

Like the teachers, they don't, and the men in bars, and the boring tax guys or finance guys who are always the ones it seems that end up chatting me up, they don't

But you. You do. You make me

So it's not that I don't

It's that I do. I do.

I wish you didn't come over tonight. Because I want you to be here.

So I wish you hadn't. Do you understand?

I'm trembling. I'm actually…

You're a hurricane you are.

A fucking hurricane.

And I'm gonna be the wreckage.

He goes to her. Holds her shaking hands.

She kisses him forcefully.

It's suddenly going very fast.

Pulling each other's clothes off. Touching bodies. Months of built-up tension unleashed.

Have you

FREDDIE. Yeah. I'm not a virgin.

He goes down on her.

Her mobile phone rings.

It fleetingly catches her attention from across the room but she ignores it.

You don't know how long I've thought about this.

Can I fuck you?

Diane, can I fuck you?

DIANE. Yes.

Do you have a condom?

FREDDIE. I'll pull out.

DIANE. You don't have one in your wallet or something?

FREDDIE. I'll pull out. Trust me. I've done it before.

DIANE. Okay.

They begin having sex.

The rain begins pelting the windows.

Outside somewhere a metal bin crashes to the ground or the wind slams an unlatched gate door.

FREDDIE. Does that feel good?

Diane, does that feel good?

It does but she doesn't answer.

I wanna cum inside you.

DIANE. Don't.

FREDDIE. Please.

DIANE. No.

FREDDIE. Does that feel good?

Diane, does that feel good?

Miss?

DIANE. Yes.

He continues penetrating her then suddenly stops.

FREDDIE. I came.

I came inside you.

DIANE. You what?

FREDDIE. Put your fingers inside and feel if you don't believe me.

He pulls the sweatpants back on. She remains where she is, frozen, feeling violated. Unable to move.

FREDDIE *starts eating a biscuit. He watches the rain.*

Long silence.

DIANE *exits to the bedroom.*

FREDDIE *sits on the couch, under a blanket.*

Turns on the TV. Flicks. Stops on a programme, occasionally laughs.

The phone begins to ring.

DIANE *re-emerges in a robe. Answers the phone.*

DIANE. Hello... Suzanne, hi... no, it's fine. I was awake... what?... I... sorry, I realise it must have seemed. Urgent. Me leaving a voicemail in the middle of the night. I just. It can wait till Monday. It was just about. The inset day. Sorry, I wasn't really. Thinking... I'm sure, nothing urgent. Speak Monday... goodnight.

FREDDIE. This is completely mental. Have you seen this?

He laughs at the TV.

Pause.

He gets up, starts to get dressed again in his wet clothes.

I was thinking I should probably go home. Dad'll be passed out by now. Prob have forgotten everything by the morning. Looks like it's barely raining now anyway.

But thanks for the clothes. And the biscuits.

See you on Monday I guess. (*Exits through the back sliding door.*)

Pause.

She turns on the garden light. He's gone.

She opens the back door. It's still raining, but much lighter now.

She goes outside. Lets the rain wash over her. Staring out into the darkness beyond.

End.

www.nickhernbooks.co.uk

facebook.com/nickhernbooks

twitter.com/nickhernbooks